T0209854

PSALMS AS SONNETS

S.A. JENSEN

WESTBOW
PRESS®
A DIVISION OF THOMAS NELSON
& ZONDERVAN

This book is a work of non-fiction. Unless otherwise noted, the author and the publisher
make no explicit guarantees as to the accuracy of the information contained in this book
and in some cases, names of people and places have been altered to protect their privacy.

WestBow Press books may be ordered through booksellers or by contacting:

WestBow Press
A Division of Thomas Nelson & Zondervan
1663 Liberty Drive
Bloomington, IN 47403
www.westbowpress.com
844-714-3454

Because of the dynamic nature of the Internet, any web addresses or links contained in
this book may have changed since publication and may no longer be valid. The views
expressed in this work are solely those of the author and do not necessarily reflect the
views of the publisher, and the publisher hereby disclaims any responsibility for them.

Certain stock imagery via @VectorStock.com

ISBN: 978-1-6642-4127-5 (sc)
ISBN: 978-1-6642-4126-8 (hc)
ISBN: 978-1-6642-4128-2 (e)

Library of Congress Control Number: 2021915044

Print information available on the last page.

WestBow Press rev. date: 08/27/2021

BOOK
ONE

I

How bless'ed is the man who does not walk
In the ungodly counsel of the vile,
Or stand among the sinners, does not mock,
Or sit with those who scoff while in their guile.
But his delight is in the law of God,
And on His law he meditates daylong.
For he is like a healthy tree, unflawed,
That's planted by the rivers—lush and strong.
The wicked are not so, but are like chaff
The wind drives far away and out of sight.
In judgment they won't stand, nor on behalf
Of those who congregate to do what's right.
   The righteous are watched over by the Lord,
   But ruin for the wicked—their reward.

2

Why do the nations rage and plot in vain?
And earthen kings find need to take a stand
Against the LORD and His Anointed, saying,
"Let us tear off Their chains and break each band."
The One enthroned in heaven will deride
Them; in His wrath He'll speak to them in terror:
"My King I placed on Zion to preside;
Be wise therefore, O kings, act not in error."
The LORD said unto Me, "You are my Son;
This day have I begotten You, so ask
Since Your inheritance won't be outdone;
Your rod will break each nation like a cask."
    Pay homage; kiss the Son; be His delight.
    Take refuge, or His anger you'll ignite.

3

O LORD how they increase—my countless foes!
With Absalom, my enemies abound.
As they approach, and I am in the throes,
I turn my heart to You and cry aloud.
Arise, O LORD, and save—You are my shield.
My trust, my faith, is ever in Your will.
I wake and hear the rolling thunder peal
When You, my King, depart Your holy hill.
The LORD sustains me even when I sleep.
The LORD takes all my fear; He is my glory.
The LORD is my salvation; He will keep
His blessings on His people—this, our story.
  When tempted to succumb to doom and dread,
  I turn to You, my God, You lift my head.

4

O God of righteousness, hear when I call
For You can vindicate and give relief.
You freed me from affliction and their gall;
Extend Your mercy; lift me from my grief.
How long, O sons of men, will you insult
And turn my glory into shamefulness?
And love all that is worthless and exult
The lies pursued in all your wickedness?
The LORD will hear my call, He sets apart
The faithful for Himself, and I will trust.
At night I meditate within my heart
And offer sacrifices; He is just.
  In You, O LORD, my joy shall e'er increase;
  With gladness in my heart, I sleep in peace.

5

Give ear, O Lord; come hear these words I pray,
And give attention to my cry, my King.
For in the morning, at first light of day,
I watch for You, and lift my voice to sing.
For You are not a God who takes delight
In wickedness—it cannot dwell with Thee.
The boastful cannot rise up in Your sight;
Your holiness rebuts iniquity.
But as for me, through all Your steadfast love,
I will bow down in fear; be merciful.
Into Your house I come, unworthy of
Your refuge. O Your way is beautiful.
   Your favor, Lord; Your love; and yes, Your shield,
   Are blessings for the righteous who will yield.

6

Have mercy on me, LORD, for I am weak.
Rebuke me not in anger; spare Your wrath.
My soul is greatly troubled—all is bleak;
But You, O LORD, how long upon this path?
Come turn, O LORD, and set my life ablaze
And rescue me by Your unfailing love.
In Sheol, who can offer You their praise?
In death no one proclaims You, God above.
My eye, consumed with sorrow, wastes away,
Yet my foes will depart for He has heard
My supplication cut through the affray.
My prayers have been received, yea, every word.
  My enemies will cower at His name;
    They will turn back disgraced and full of shame.

7

O Lord my God, in You I place my trust;
For my pursuers come, draw near and save,
Lest like a lion, they, in their disgust,
Will tear my soul to pieces to my grave.
If this injustice is upon my hands,
If I have done this wrong to one at peace,
Repaid my friend with evil-hearted plans,
Then may he tread me down; my days will cease.
You are my shield who saves the upright heart.
God is a righteous judge who, in His ire,
Will bend His bow, and aim each fiery dart
At those who won't repent—whose straits are dire.
   Yet I will praise the Lord, whose righteousness
   Is worthy of my songs of thankfulness.

8

Majestic is Your name, O LORD, our Lord.
Above the heavens, You have set Your glory
In all the earth; Your name can't be ignored;
Your majesty declares Your wondrous story.
When I observe Your heavens placed above,
The pale moon and the stars—works of Your fingers,
Then what is man, the son of man You love,
That You remember him—or that he lingers?
Yet You created him a little lower
Than God and placed upon his head a crown.
You made him lord of all Your works—a sower
Of all beneath his feet upon Your ground.
   Majestic is Your name, O LORD, our Lord;
   Throughout the earth Your name shall be adored.

9

What refuge is the LORD for all oppressed;
He is a shelter in our times of trouble.
Forgotten not are those who are distressed;
For all who cry for help among the rubble.
Be gracious, LORD, consider my complaint,
And lift me from these dreadful gates of death.
For those who hate me chained me in restraints.
Come rescue me; I'll praise You with each breath.
For when my enemies turn and retreat,
They stumble and they perish in Your sight.
For You upheld my cause, condemned deceit,
And never will abandon the upright.
  With all my heart I sing and lift Your name;
  With thankful hearts we sing of Your great fame.

10

O Lord, why do You stand so far away?
In troubled times, why do You hide from men?
In arrogance, the wicked plot their way;
Let them be taken in their schemes—amen.
"There is no God," he says within his heart,
He schemes as if the Lord does not exist.
His mouth is full of fraud; he will depart
To hide, then harm the poor with his cruel fist.
Arise, O Lord; O God, lift up Your hand;
The helper of the poor and fatherless.
Remove the nations from Your precious land,
Our King, forever, God of righteousness.
   You hear all humble hearts when they implore
   That men of earth may terrify no more.

II

Enshrouded in the dark, the wicked hide.
They bend their bows; their arrows have been nocked.
They lie in wait to kill with guile and pride,
To shoot the saints with upright hearts they've stalked.
What can the righteous do if they destroy
The strong foundations set upon the earth?
Flee to the mountain? Give in to their ploy?
Fly like a bird? Or lay aside their worth?
The LORD resides in heaven on His throne.
He tests the righteous; yea, He sees each man.
He hates the wicked; He will not condone
Their acts of violence they plot and plan.
    The LORD loves righteous deeds; He will embrace
    The upright, who will look upon His face.

12

Come help, O LORD, the godly were replaced
With liars who deceive with hearts awry.
The loyal, lost; humanity disgraced;
What's true has been distorted with a lie.
The LORD will silence every boastful tongue
That flatters to advance a selfish way.
"With words we'll reign; we'll climb up every rung;
For who is master over us?" they say.
The LORD will come; He'll free us from the vile;
The wicked prowl, but Yahweh will provide.
"Because the poor are suffering in their trial,
I will arise—in safety they may hide."
    His words will stand forever; truth defined
    Like purest silver—seven times refined.

13

How long will You forget me, LORD? How long?
Console me while I wait in readiness.
You hide Your face, yet I give You this song
With sorrow in my heart; I long for rest.
My enemy's exalted over me.
How long will You be silent? Not a breath?
Consider me and answer this, my plea:
Light up my eyes lest I sleep to my death.
But I have trusted in Your steadfast love;
My heart takes joy in Your deliverance.
My enemies will turn, unworthy of
Salvation; they embrace belligerence.
   For unto You, my LORD, will my heart sing;
    You've given much to me, my God and King.

14

"There is no God," the fool says in his heart.
They are corrupt, not one does what is good.
Their actions are revolting—all depart
From God—pursuing evil and falsehood.
The LORD looks down from heaven on mankind
To see if there are those who understand;
If there is one who seeks Him, one inclined
To welcome mercy from His loving hand.
Yet all have turned aside, all are corrupt.
There is none who does good, not even one.
Consuming souls like bread, the vile disrupt
The poor—yet they'll see terror when undone.
   The righteous find a refuge in the LORD,
   And Jacob will rejoice when they're restored.

15

O LORD, who shall dwell on Your holy hill?
And in Your tent, what soul can so abide?
What must a man, O LORD, do to fulfill
What You require to be justified?
Walk blamelessly and e'er do what is right,
And speak the truth—your tongue should slander not.
Don't take reproach against your friend in spite,
And keep your word without a second thought.
And honor those who fear and love the LORD,
And love not what surrounds the foul and vile.
Be generous with money; never hoard
Or bribe against the innocent with guile.
   The one with guilty hands will not be moved;
   O LORD, who shall be holy and approved?

16

I say unto the LORD, You are my Lord;
For I have nothing good apart from You.
Abundant joy when we're in one accord;
Protect me, God, my refuge is in You.
Your path of life revealed, by love, to me,
The boundary lines delightfully are drawn.
Indeed, I have a pleasant place to be;
My beautiful inheritance will dawn.
My heart is glad the LORD comes to advise.
And still, at night, His counsel does not sleep.
But those who chase false gods seek their demise;
I will not join them as their sorrows heap.
  Corruption will not touch Your Holy One.
  My soul will not see Sheol; He has won.

17

You come by night, my life is Yours to see.
You test my heart and motives held within.
I hold fast to Your paths You have for me;
My mouth, I have determined, will not sin.
Attend my cry and let my voice be heard,
And closely listen to what my heart sings.
My enemies surround me; fears are stirred.
Come hide me 'neath the shadow of Your wings.
I call upon You, God, You will respond
And rise against my adversary's hate.
The apple of Your eye, of me You're fond.
Arise, O Lord! I'll trust You as I wait.
    When I awake and see Your holy face,
    My anxiousness will leave without a trace.

18

I love You, Lord, You are my strength and shield,
And my deliverer; You are my rock.
The horn of my salvation, I'm concealed
In You, my mighty tower, help me walk.
I called unto the Lord in my distress,
Unto my faithful God I cried His name.
He heard me from His temple, I profess,
Upon a soaring cherub, Yahweh came.
Transcendent roar of heaven, earth it shook;
On wings of wind to save He came apace.
Delighted in His king, the Lord betook
To rescue me and grant a spacious place.
  Unbounded love the Lord gives unto me.
  To David He has shown His loyalty.

19

The skies declare the glory of our God.
His handiwork is shown in heav'n above.
His message, though not heard, is cast abroad—
Pours forth His knowledge rooted in His love.
The perfect law of God revives my soul;
His testimony, sure, and makes me wise;
His righteous statutes gladden my heart whole;
Commands are bright, enlightening my eyes.
The fear of God is pure, fore'er endures.
His judgments are but right and ever true,
And worth far more than gold for He assures
A great reward, when keeping them, shines through.
  O that the meditation of my heart
  And spoken words, would love for Thee impart.

20

May answers come when troubled days arrive;
Be hedged within the name of Jacob's God.
His help from sanctuary to revive,
From Zion, strength—'tis Yahweh whom we laud.
May heaven's answers satisfy your heart
And plans fulfilled sown of the Spirit's seed.
We shout for joy; salvation He'll impart
For by His hand anointed ones take heed.
Yet in the end the chariots will rust,
And mightiest of horses come up lame,
But in the name of LORD our God we trust:
Give victory to the king; we trust Your name.
   For those who doubt the LORD collapse and fall.
   O Yahweh, may You answer when we call.

21

The king rejoices in Your strength, O Lord,
And greatly he exults Your victory.
His heart's desire given—not ignored;
Your presence gives him joy eternally.
A crown of gold You placed upon his head;
Rich blessings You bestowed upon Your king.
He asked for length of days, for life he pled;
Your majesty and splendor make him sing.
For You will capture all Your enemies,
Uprooting souls who hate You with Your hand.
A fiery furnace waits for those You seize—
Your wrath upon the wicked in the land.
    O Lord, come be exalted in Your might;
    We sing and praise Your power and Your light.

22

Why have You, God, forsaken Me? O why?
Why are You far from My deliverance
And all My words of groaning? You deny
My cry for rest at night—indifference?
Yet You are holy, high upon the throne
On Israel's words of praise and songs of grace.
Our fathers placed their trust in You alone;
They cried to You; You freed them from disgrace.
With pierce'ed hands and feet, My blood is shed;
They cast lots for My clothing; hear My cry.
Yet I will give You praise and look ahead;
The humble You will feed and satisfy.
   Declare to all the victory has been won;
   Proclaim the righteous deeds our God has done.

23

My shepherd is the LORD; I shall not want.
In fields of green the LORD makes me lie down.
By quiet waters walks my confidant,
Where He restores my soul to His renown.
He leads me on His paths of righteousness,
Revealing prudent steps for me to take,
Anoints my head with oil—His lavishness
All done in love, fulfilled for His name's sake.
My soul is comforted under His care,
Though valley of death's shadow looms ahead.
A table 'round my enemies prepared,
By rod and staff, Your lamb shall fear no dread.
  My cup o'erflows, and mercy follows me,
  And in Your house I'll live eternally.

24

He founded earth on rivers and on seas.
Inhabitants are His by His design;
Sublime creation shouts His majesty,
New mercies granted from the One divine.
Ascend His holy mountain—how can we?
Majestic crest of God—for us to stand?
Elect to never swear deceitfully;
Ignore all falsehood; muse on His commands.
Salvation comes for those whose hands are clean;
Just, King of glory, purify our hearts.
Eternal blessings shall, in time, be seen;
Strong is our LORD; His glory ne'er departs.
 Unlock the gates and open ancient doors!
 Shout to the King of glory, He's the LORD!

25

In You, O LORD my God, I place my trust.
I lift my soul; in You my hope shall rest.
Come keep me far from shame and the unjust;
Let not my enemies see me oppressed.
For none who wait for You will be disgraced,
But for the treacherous, disgrace appears.
Show me Your ways; Your truth I have embraced.
You are the God and Savior my heart fears.
Forgive my sin, O LORD, for it is great;
For Your name's sake, forgive iniquity.
I am afflicted, LORD, come and abate
The troubles of my heart; deliver me.
   With eagerness I wait and watch for You.
   Redeem good Israel; give him hope anew.

26

O vindicate me, LORD, for I have walked
In my integrity; in You I trust.
Come test my heart and mind; my life's unlocked
For You to prove and try me; You are just.
With men of falsehood I will not consort,
Or sit with hypocrites in their ill fame.
I hate how wayward crowds meet to exhort
Those evildoers who reject Your name.
O LORD, I love the place where You reside;
The place where I can find Your wondrous glory.
Don't sweep my soul away with those in pride;
Those men of bloodshed—evil is their story.
   But I shall walk in my integrity.
   My foot's on level ground and e'er shall be.

27

The LORD is my salvation and my light;
Whom shall I fear with You before my eyes?
You are my stronghold; stay within my sight.
To gaze on beauty, Thine, a brilliant prize.
In faith, Your servant has this certainty,
For all my days I've sought Your holy face,
While in the land of th'living I will see
The blessing of Your goodness in this place.
But now I face the evil at my door;
Adversity has come, it is the day.
Conceal me, LORD, and hear me, I implore,
And hide me 'neath Thy cover—don't delay.
  O be courageous, let your heart be strong;
  Come wait upon the LORD and sing this song.

28

To You, O LORD, I call; please hear my prayer.
If You were deaf to me I could not stand.
Forever I would be in deep despair—
To misery I'd succumb without Your hand.
I call aloud for mercy with my voice.
Toward sanctuary, Thine, I lift my hands
In praise. My Rock, I cry to You; rejoice
For You have heard my cry; Your mercy stands.
With evil hearts the wicked smile and nod
At neighbors to deceive. The peace they speak
Is rooted in contempt. How they mock God.
Come bring them down and vindicate the meek.
　　O LORD, You are our strength; You are our shield.
　　Exultant hearts are hearts that trust and yield.

29

The God of glory thunders—hear His voice.
The cedars split beneath the mighty din.
Above the waters, hearken and rejoice;
Reverberation shaketh all within.
The voice of Yahweh flashes flames of fire
And quakes the Kadesh wilderness to core.
The woodlands stripped, the deer in labor—dire,
When God and His majestic voice doth roar.
Ascribe to God His glory and His might.
Ascribe to God the glory due His name.
His holiness unequalled, none as bright
As Yahweh, King forever, we proclaim.
    The LORD, enthroned, will give His people peace.
    Be blessed, receive His strength, your fears will cease.

30

I will extol You, LORD, You've drawn me up
And have not let my foes rejoice o'er me.
I cried to You for help to fill my cup.
You healed me, LORD, when I called unto Thee.
I thank the LORD, who spared me from the pit,
And praise His holy name to my delight.
The joy of morning comes when we submit,
Enduring any weeping in the night.
I sing to You, my LORD, and give You praise.
With morning came Your joy with mere a glance.
Your mercy lifts my heart—'tis set ablaze,
And now my mourning's turned into a dance.
    For I will not be silent, I will sing—
    Forever giving praise to God, my King.

31

O be a rock of refuge for me, LORD;
Incline Your ear, and save me speedily.
You are my fortress; You are my reward.
Come lead and guide me; Your name sets me free.
Into Your hands, my spirit I commit.
I trust in You, rejoicing in Your love.
For You have known my troubles; I submit,
Come lift me by Your mercy high above.
And in a spacious place You set my feet.
I trust in You; my times are in Your hand.
Though grief and anguish come, I will entreat
You and Your goodness; You will help me stand.
  Be strong and be courageous as you wait,
  All you who place your hope in God the great.

32

O bless'ed is the man whose sin is covered;
The one who is forgiven, blessed is he.
And bless'ed is the one who has discovered
The One who counts not his iniquity.
For when Your hand was heavy on my back,
My strength was gone; I groaned all day and night.
Acknowledging my sin, I saw my lack:
"I will confess my sin; I am contrite."
Let everyone trust in the LORD and pray
For He will be your rescue; turn to Him.
You are my hiding place; You show my way,
And You surround me with this joyful hymn.
  How blessed is he who knows his sins are gone.
  How blessed are we for unto Him we're drawn.

33

We wait upon the LORD, our hearts rejoice
And trust His holy name and steadfast love.
For earthly kings and armies have no voice
When likened to the matchless God above.
A warrior, though strong, will always fail,
And horses in their might are but false hope.
For only help from faithful God prevails
As nothing is beyond His righteous scope.
He forged the radiant stars with but a breath,
And by a word were brilliant heavens made.
For His command delivers one from death
Who fears the LORD—and to the LORD hath prayed.
   We offer Him a new song, and we shout.
   Our hearts with His, He casts away all doubt.

34

O Yahweh, when I made my urgent plea
And sought You when my heart was full of fear,
Your radiance from Your presence covered me.
My troubles went away when You appeared.
The angel of the LORD encamped around
Your servant when afraid and when alone.
I cried unto the LORD; yea, I was found.
His eyes are on the righteous; I am known.
For when the brokenhearted turn and pray
With spirits crushed, He hears with love profound.
Afflictions of the righteous bring dismay,
Yet God's deliverance shall e'er abound.
   My soul will ever boast in You, O LORD.
   Your holy name will ever be adored.

35

Keep not Your silence, Lord, and be not far.
Awaken, God, and rise to my defense.
False witnesses approach; my name they mar.
Your vindication bring—and recompense.
Let them be put to shame, all those who say,
"We have devoured him"—a ruthless claim.
Like profane mockers at a feast, they prey
And gnash their teeth at me in their ill fame.
Let those who long for virtue shout for joy:
"The Lord shall be exalted"—let us state.
The many who have gathered to destroy
My life find wrath as their deserv'ed fate.
    Lord, Your deliverance is my delight.
    My tongue shall tell of You and of Your might.

36

Your steadfast love will to the heavens reach;
Your faithfulness up to the clouds above.
Your righteousness like highest mountain peaks;
Your judgments like the deepest seas thereof.
For underneath the shadow of Your wings,
The children of mankind come place their trust.
They're filled with the abundance Your house brings.
Your light, their light; Your fountain is robust.
Yet sin speaks to the wicked in his heart;
There is no fear of God before his eyes.
While on his bed he plots an evil chart;
He will not turn from evil or from lies.
   The evil cannot rise; they are thrust down.
   They cannot hide their sin, in sin they'll drown.

37

Be still before the Lord; with patience, wait.
Commit your way to Him, and He will act.
Turn from your evil; trust, for He makes straight
Your path into the land the Lord has mapped.
Refrain from anger, and give up your rage
For agitation only hands you harm.
The Lord will help; His justice will assuage
Your troubled heart; the wicked He'll disarm.
For yet a little while they will remain,
But wicked men and wickedness will cease.
Wait for the Lord, and keep His way again.
There is a future for the man of peace.
  Delight yourself in Him; be set apart.
  He'll give you the desires of your heart.

38

The burden of my sin I cannot bear,
And my iniquities confound my rest.
Your arrows sink in me, LORD, I'm aware
Of how my foolishness dashed what was best.
Depravity, a flood that's o'er my head—
I'm drowning in a life I once enjoyed.
I cannot see or hear; I'm left for dead.
I writhe in pain; of health I am devoid.
Please be not far; Your truth is what I love.
My life I lay before You—torn apart.
I'm feeble; I have roared by reason of
Disquietness abounding in my heart.
　　Do not abandon me, O Lord, make haste.
　　Do not be far; don't let me be disgraced.

39

The brevity of life confounds You not,
For all mankind at best is vanity.
We amble forth like shadows, oft are fraught
With efforts to gain wealth, inanity.
Reveal my end; come measure all my days.
How frail am I, how fleeting is my span.
In silence my heart burns; I guard my ways.
My sorrow's stirred for I am but a man.
O hear my prayer; give ear unto my cry.
Hold not Your peace; Your silence I deplore.
Like fathers 'fore me, hear this stranger's sigh,
And spare Your servant 'fore I am no more.
   Deliver me from sin—this is my plea.
   For You, God, are my hope; I wait for Thee.

40

I waited patiently upon the LORD;
In mercy He inclined and heard my cry.
What joy to know my voice was not ignored
When lifted from the pit and set on high.
A new song has been given unto me—
A hymn of praise to sing to worthy God.
Great multitudes will hear and trust and see
The LORD is whom we seek and fear and laud.
Your thoughts are us-ward, countless though they be,
They're wondrous like Your deeds; none can compare.
I will proclaim and tell of them. You'll see
My heart delights to do Your will with care.
  I am afflicted, yet You think of me.
  You shall deliver; come, Lord, set me free.

41

The LORD protects and keeps alive the one
Considering the poor, the souls in need.
For when a time of trouble has begun,
The generous will see Him intercede.
The LORD will bless his life while in the land
And will not hand him to his enemy.
While on his sickbed, God will help him stand
And heal him of his dire infirmity.
Be merciful to me for I have sinned
Against You, LORD, draw nigh and raise me up.
My friends have turned against me like the wind;
They whisper of their poison in my cup.
   But even when a trusted friend betrays,
   Our God delivers; ever give Him praise.

BOOK
TWO

42

The deer longs for the water as my soul
Pants for You, God, pants for the living God.
I thirst for Him and long for Him to show
Me when I can appear without facade.
For I recall my joyful walks with friends
Up to the house of God to seek His face.
Our voices full of praise, songs would ascend
To God, whose faithful love is full of grace.
So why am I cast down and full of dread?
Disquiet in this heart that once knew peace?
And all the waves and billows o'er my head
For deep will call to deep; O let it cease.
    Though in the storm, through darkness I still grope,
    I will praise God and place in Him my hope.

43

O vindicate me, God, defend my cause,
And rescue me from the deceitful man.
Send out Your light and truth without a pause,
And lead me to Your holy hill again.
And in Your tabernacle I can mourn
My enemies' oppression 'fore Your throne.
Don't cast me off; come turn away Your scorn,
And strengthen me to face what is unknown.
For with my lyre, this music I enjoy,
I reach Your altar, God, to give You praise.
You are my God and my exceeding joy.
My God alone delivers, loves, and saves.
  For when my soul is downcast I will cope
  By praising God; in Him I place my hope.

44

O God, our ears have heard the tales of old;
Our fathers shared what wondrous works Thou didst.
Your hand drove out the nations, we were told,
Afflicting enemies found in their midst.
Their land was granted, God, not by their sword,
Nor did their arm give them a victory.
But Your right hand, Your arm, allowed reward;
Your light, Your face, Your mercy set them free.
O God, You are my King, deliver us
For I will not trust in my sword or bow
As my efforts are but superfluous.
For victory is Yours—of this I know.
    Arise and wake, our souls cling to the dust.
    In Your unfailing love we place our trust.

45

My heart wells over with a noble theme;
My tongue writes like a ready scribe for I
Address these verses to a noble King;
For You are bless'ed by our God, for aye.
Now gird Your mighty sword upon Your side.
Humility and justice stir Your cause;
In majesty and glory You will ride.
Your throne will last forever without pause.
Your arrows pierce the hearts of enemies.
You love what's righteous; wickedness You spoil.
Your righteous scepter levies penalties.
And God, Your God, has blessed Your head with oil.
  With gladness and rejoicing, saints will sing
  As they approach the palace of the King.

46

God is our refuge and our strength; fear not.
Although the earth gives way and mountains fall
Into the depths, and all we know is fraught,
A very present help in trouble calls.
Though nations rage and kingdoms are inane,
A refuge waits; His strength is always there.
Though fear cries out amid the war and pain,
Still Jacob's God awaits to loose each snare.
There is a river in the holy place;
Its streams delight God's city, and upon
The holy dwelling of His love and grace,
Our God will help her when the morning dawns.
   Be still, and know that I am God, e'er will,
    And e'er know that I am your God, be still.

47

We shout to God, and clap for He is King;
Triumphant voices shout throughout the land.
And praises to our God, the nations sing
For He subdued our foes on whom we stand.
The LORD, Most High, our King, is to be feared;
Provision He will choose for those He loves.
Unto the pride of Jacob, love appeared.
Sing praises with a psalm to God above!
Amid the shouts, our mighty God ascends
Above the nations in their lowliness.
Sing to a mighty King whose love ne'er ends,
Who rises to His throne of holiness.
　　The nobles of the nations come to praise
　　As Abraham's dear people, hearts ablaze.

48

For in His city, God, our LORD, is great,
And greatly to be praised. His holy peak
Ascends with splendor; all will venerate
The city of the King of whom we seek.
Mount Zion rests on slopes found to the north;
Encircle it, and tour its citadels.
Take note and count its ramparts and go forth.
"Our God will lead us"; go ye now and tell.
Behold, the kings assembled have advanced.
They looked and froze in fear—in terror, fled.
Their ships were wrecked by Thee; did they recant?
Rebellion 'gainst our God will lead to dread.
    Just as we heard, our God forever reigns.
    Just as we saw in Zion, God remains.

49

Hear this, all people of the world, give ear.
Both rich and poor and high and low take heed.
My mouth will utter wisdom; gather near,
And understand this proverb and this creed.
For those who trust in wealth romance a lie
As riches cannot e'er redeem a friend,
Nor give to God a ransom to comply;
One cannot buy redemption in the end.
Like sheep they are appointed to the grave.
Yea death shall be their shepherd to the pit.
Boast not of riches; lies will e'er enslave
All they who trust in wealth o'er holy writ.
　For God put forth a plan to conquer death.
　Redemption is a gift while we have breath.

50

The Mighty One, our LORD, from Zion speaks
And summons earth from east unto the west.
A tempest rages 'round Him which bespeaks
His holiness as fire precedes His quest.
Unto the faithful, God speaks to proclaim,
"Your sacrifices I will not reject.
But know I own the hills and own the game;
Your thankfulness—take care to not neglect."
And to the wicked, God lifts up His voice:
"My covenant was never in your heart.
You have rejected Me, and made your choice:
Forget your God and you'll be torn apart."
　　For sacrifices offered to defraud
　　Will fail to earn salvation from our God.

51

Have mercy on me, God, cleanse me from sin.
According to the steadfast love You've shown,
Come wash away iniquity within
This heart that turned against You, You alone.
Your judgment's justified and without blame.
In sin I was conceived, behold, since birth.
Within me You desire truth, not shame,
And there You teach me wisdom by Your worth.
With hyssop, purge and wash me, make me clean;
Forever I will be whiter than snow.
And let me hear a gladness unforeseen,
My broken and repentant heart You know.
  Create in me a clean heart—set me free,
  Renew a steadfast spirit within me.

52

Why do you boast of evil, mighty man?
And rather than speak truth, you utter lies?
Why do you plot destruction when you can
Turn to enduring goodness and be wise?
"This man chose not to make our God his strength,
But trusted in his riches and his vice.
Rejecting God has led him into angst,
Out of the land, uprooted—a dear price."
But I am like a thriving olive tree.
God's steadfast love I'll trust fore'er and e'er.
And I will offer praise and thanks to Thee.
Your faithful people join me in this prayer.
   I place my hope in You, Your name is great.
   I place in You my trust, and I will wait.

53

The fool says in his heart, "There is no God."
Corrupt are they, and vile, for none are good.
Encumbered by iniquity they plod
On earth while never living as they should.
Yet God looks down from heaven for the wise
Among the human race, for one who seeks
His face—but all are filthy; all despise
Instruction and don't hearken when He speaks.
But there they are in terror, in their dread,
When terror is not nigh to give them fear.
For those who were besieging them are dead.
Our God despised them; they're no longer near.
   When God frees all held captive and restores,
   Then Jacob will rejoice upon his shores.

54

O listen to my words, and hear my prayer.
Come save me by Your name and by Your might.
For strangers rise against me—be aware;
God, vindicate me, set all things aright.
Oppressors come who know You not, my God.
Repay my adversaries for their harm.
Your justice, faithful, with Thy staff and rod.
My enemies cut off with Your strong arm.
A freewill offering I sacrifice.
I praise Your name, O LORD, for it is good.
Those evil, out to harm, held in Your vice,
See justice that is right and understood.
   From every trouble He delivered me.
   I look in triumph o'er my enemy.

55

My heart is full of anguish o'er his voice.
I'm overwhelmed; I tremble in my fear.
If I could wander off on wings—rejoice!
Then fly away, would I, from dearth and drear.
This raging wind and storm are deep within,
Oppression more than I can comprehend.
While torment I expect from those in sin,
I cannot bear betrayal by a friend.
My cries are heard; God hears each time I call—
Sustains me and delivers me unmarred.
My enemy's afflicted, and will fall
With war within his heart, a heart that's hard.
  His speech, as smooth as butter, was a sword;
    Come trust—and cast your burden on the Lord.

56

Be gracious unto me, I am afraid.
My enemies oppress me all day long
To trample and to harm and to degrade;
Their evil thoughts against me are but wrong.
Together they assemble, and they hide.
My steps they mark; they wait to take my soul.
For their iniquity cast them aside.
Your justice and Your mercy I extol.
Your word, O God, I praise; Your word I praise.
O Lord, in You I trust and will not fear
What can man do; O God, I trust Your ways.
From death I am set free; You I revere.
    My tears are in Your bottle and Your book.
    I'll walk before You; in Your light I'll look.

57

Be merciful to me, O God, please hear
My prayer; O God, be merciful to me.
For in the shadow of Your wings be near,
And refuge take, my soul that trusts in Thee.
And when the storms surround me, heed my call;
My heart cries out for help—'tis God I trust.
Come send Your help from heaven when I fall,
When evil tramples me into the dust.
Among the lions and the fiery beasts,
My soul takes comfort in the one true God.
From heaven, a transcendent sense of peace.
I lie down and awake—I'm safe and awed.
   Awake, my glory! Praise I'll cast upon
   My God in heaven; I'll awake the dawn!

58

Do you indeed command with righteousness?
And do you fairly judge with upright hearts?
Or is your justice mere capriciousness,
Determined not by scales and not by charts.
The wicked go astray but from the womb,
And liars err from birth—e'er to deceive.
Like poison from the adder, words entomb
The innocent when lies are yet believed.
Come break their teeth, God, in their mouths that lie.
Tear out the fangs of lions who do harm.
Come blunt their arrows aimed to fill the sky;
Your retribution comes from Your strong arm.
   The righteous will then say, "There is reward;
   There is One who will judge—He is the Lord."

59

I call on God for my deliverance;
My wicked enemies have risen up.
Keep me from those who clutch irreverence,
Dark men of bloodshed lurk to fill their cup.
By night they snarl and prowl and howl like dogs.
Their strident speech spews out of lips like swords.
The scattered, by Your hand, wander and slog,
But kill them not; yet give their just rewards.
And of Your mercy and Your pow'r I sing.
At daybreak I will joyfully proclaim
You are my fortress—unto You I cling;
'Tis steadfast love I find within Your name.
   You are my strength on whom I can rely.
   I sing and praise Your steadfast love; draw nigh.

60

O God, You have rejected us; relent.
Repair us, God, for we are broken still.
Your hand has quaked the land, and we repent.
Come heal its breach; restore us if You will.
We're staggered by the wine You had us drink,
Yet You sent up a flag for all who fear.
They flee before the archers—You they seek.
With Your right hand come save us and draw near.
And in Your holiness we heard You speak:
"I will rejoice! I will divide the land!
For it is Mine—all valleys and each peak."
Deliver those You love; come help us stand.
   All help from men is vain; we need You, God.
   Defeat our enemies for we are flawed.

61

Attend unto my prayer, O God, and hear
My cry I send from the end of the earth.
My heart is overwhelmed, O God, give ear—
Lead to the higher rock; Your joy, Your mirth.
For You have been a refuge for the king,
A tower that is strong before my foes.
And refuge I will take under Your wing;
And in Your tent I'll live while in the throes.
Appoint Your faithful love and truth to guard.
I will abide before You while enthroned
To ever sing Your praises and regard
Your name, O God, Your holy name alone.
  As I perform my vows I give You praise,
  A heritage to hold You in my gaze.

62

In silence my soul waits for God alone;
My hope and my salvation are at hand.
He is my fortress and my rock—atones
For sins; I am not shaken—here I stand.
Though some will plot and scheme to take man down,
And batter like a leaning fence or wall,
Yet in their lies and falsehood will they drown
And curse they, inward—downward they will fall.
For He has spoken once, twice have I heard,
That strength belongs to God—and steadfast love.
You render unto man, yea I have heard,
According to his works You see above.
    If wealth increases, give it not your trust.
    Pour out your heart before Him; He is just.

63

O God, You are my God; 'tis You I seek.
In weary and dry lands I thirst for You.
Your steadfast love is what my lips shall speak.
My flesh is faint, yet You make things anew.
Your power and Your glory I have seen
Within Your sanctuary scores of days.
As long as I have life we will convene,
And in Your holy name, I'll give You praise.
And on night's watch, enshrouded by the dark,
I meditate on You and follow close.
Your right hand will uphold as I embark
To watch the sword bring low all who oppose.
  For in the mighty shadow of Your wings,
   I lift my hands, and to You my heart sings.

64

Come hear my voice, O God, hear my complaints.
Preserve my life; my enemies bring dread.
They talk of laying snares to trap the saints;
With tongues as swords, their bitter words are said.
Injustice they search out with diligence;
In inward thoughts of men contempt will seep.
Come hide me, God, and rise to my defense,
For You know that the hearts of men are deep.
Without forewarning, God will bend His bow.
He'll shoot to wound; His arrows meet their mark.
They're brought to ruin; God will e'er bring low
The wicked who rouse fear; He casts out dark.
   Take refuge, all you righteous, and give praise.
   Rejoice and give God glory all our days.

65

All praise is due to You, O God, in Zion,
And unto You our vows shall be performed.
O You who hears our prayers beneath Orion,
Atonement comes from You; we are reformed.
O God, You are our hope and our salvation
For all across the earth—from distant seas.
For by Your power You set fast each mountain.
You're robed with strength; You bring us to our knees.
You visit earth and soften it with showers.
Your river's full of water; You give grain.
The pastures, clothed with flocks, show Your great powers;
The valleys shout in triumph—lift Your name.
  Our God, who stills the roaring of the sea,
  Will calm the storm that rages within me.

66

Shout joyfully to God, all of the earth!
Sing forth the honor of His glorious name!
How awesome are Your works and great Your worth.
Your enemies submit unto Your fame.
O come and see the works our God has done
For He has turned the sea into dry land.
And through the flood on foot, forsaking none,
Delivered us; we praise His mighty hand.
Come listen all who fear the Lord our God,
And I will tell what He has done for me.
Through fire and through water we have trod,
Refined as silver, given much, set free.
   Praise God, He has not turned away my prayer.
   His love was not withheld without a care.

67

May God be ever merciful to us,
And make His face to shine upon us all.
Come bless us that Your ways be known, we trust
Your saving pow'r, among all nations, calls.
O God let all the people give You praise.
Let everyone exalt You, God above.
And sing for joy, the nations You have raised,
With righteous judgments given forth in love.
The earth has yielded increase; it is blessed
By God, our God, whose blessings do appear
Across the earth, from east unto the west.
Let all the nations look to Him with fear.
   And let Your face, O God, on us come shine.
   We praise the righteous judgments that are Thine.

68

Let God arise; His enemies disperse;
Let those who hate Him flee before His eyes.
Like smoke is blown away, so the perverse
Will drift and melt like wax to their demise.
O God, when You went out before all men,
And through the wilderness You rode and marched,
You shook the earth, poured rain upon the glen,
Cared for the poor, yet rebel land was parched.
Come sing to God, you kingdoms of the earth,
And sing to Him who thunders with His voice.
Ascribe to God His power and His worth;
His strength is in the clouds—to Him, rejoice!
  The God of Israel gives His people power;
  His strength He gives His people every hour.

69

O save me, God, up to my neck doth rise
The waters, overflowing where I stand.
While waiting for Your help, so fail my eyes.
In mire I am sinking; give Your hand.
Please answer me, O LORD, Your love is good.
According to Your mercy, turn to me.
Draw nigh unto my soul; on You I've stood.
Hide not Your face, and hear me speedily.
My heart is wounded, broken by reproach,
And full of heaviness, shame, and despair.
I turn to You; I wait for Your approach.
In Your abundant mercy hear my prayer.
   Let Your salvation, God, set me on high.
   With grateful hymns, Your name I'll magnify.

70

Make haste, O God, come now; deliver me
From those who seek my life—put them to shame.
Let them turn back; confuse them; set me free;
Bring them to their dishonor; hear my claim.
For they take pleasure in my misery;
They say "Aha! Aha!" They wish me pain.
My enemies make light of what they see;
When I am low, they treat me with disdain.
May all who seek You find You and be glad.
May they rejoice, all they who seek and wait.
May those who love salvation come unclad
Of pride and say forever, "God is great!"
   But I am poor and needy and disgraced;
   Deliver me; You are my help, make haste.

71

I place my trust in You, O Lord, and walk,
And in Your righteousness deliver me.
For You, Lord, are my fortress and my rock;
My mouth is full of praise I offer Thee.
Deliver me, O God, out of the hands
Of wicked and cruel men who mean me harm.
You are my hope; I trust in Your commands
For from the womb I've leaned upon Your arm.
Calamities and troubles I have seen
For You allowed misfortune o'er my days.
But You will lift me up; You shall redeem.
Your faithfulness, O God, worthy of praise.
  O Holy One of Israel, I will sing.
  My lips rejoice; my praise an offering.

72

O may the mountains bring prosperity,
And let the hills attend by righteousness.
Defend the poor, deliver charity;
Redeem them from oppression and distress.
And may it be, while sun and moon endure,
Your reign continue, like the rain will fall
Upon cut grass—like showers on the moor.
O may the righteous flourish by your call.
And let there be abundance on the land.
May there be grain and fruit; let it abound.
And while his cities flourish and expand,
His enemies lick dust upon the ground.
  O God of Israel, bless'ed be Your name.
  The earth and sun will manifest Your fame.

BOOK
THREE

73

Our God is good to those whose hearts are pure.
But as for me, I nearly went astray
As I envied the arrogant, unsure
Of why the wicked prospered in their way.
They have a painless life until their death.
They are not plagued with strife like others, hence
Their pride encompasses as close as breath.
Their eyes are bulging out in corpulence.
Yet whom have I in heaven, God, but Thee?
Besides You there are none whom I desire.
My flesh and heart may fail inside of me,
But in God's presence, I am taken higher.
    For I have taken refuge in the Lord
    That I may tell the world of my reward.

74

Why have You cast us off forever, God?
Why does Your anger smoke against Your sheep?
Recall Your congregation and Your rod
Of Your inheritance for You to keep.
And give, O God, Your covenant regard.
The darker places of the earth are cruel.
Put not to shame the downcast and the marred.
Arise against the slander of the fool.
Do not forget the clamor of Your foes,
The outcry of the ones who rise against.
Defend Your cause against all who oppose.
Arise, my King of old, it has commenced.
　　Among us none no when; we see no sign.
　　The day and night and moon and sun are Thine.

75

"For I will judge with equity in time;
I say unto the boastful, 'do not boast.'
I say unto the wicked in their crime,
'Lift not your horn, with necks stiff as a post.'"
Promotion comes not from the east nor west,
But God, the Judge, will choose whom will arise.
Nor exaltation from the wilderness.
God lifts one up, sends one to his demise.
For in the hand of God there is a cup.
The wine is red, well-mixed; He pours from it.
The wicked of the earth on it will sup,
And drink the dregs thereof—for it is writ.
   Unto the God of Jacob, I sing praise.
   With justice He shall choose which ones to raise.

76

In Judah, God is known; His name is great
In Israel. Salem set, victorious
His tabernacle, and His dwelling state
In Zion. You, our God, are glorious.
And there He broke the arrows of the bow,
The shield, the sword, the weaponry of war.
And You are far more excellent, we know,
Than mountains full of prey; You we adore.
When God arose to judge, the meek to save,
The stouthearted were plundered, put to sleep.
The men of war unhanded; none were brave
When chariots were cast into a heap.
  Our awe-inspiring God, our gifts we bring.
  Our God is to be feared by every king.

77

I cry aloud to God, and He will hear.
This day of trouble, I shall seek the Lord.
At night, with lifted hands, He will give ear.
My spirit faints; my heart has been outpoured.
Your ancient wonders, Lord, I will recall,
And meditate on works of Your own hand.
Your way is holy; nothing could befall
To match Your strength revealed across Your land.
The waters saw You, God, and were afraid;
The clouds above poured rain upon the ground.
The crash of thunder rolled above the glade;
The arrows filled the sky with light profound.
　Your way is in the sea, as is Your path,
　Your footsteps unseen in the aftermath.

78

Incline your ears, O people, to my words.
My mouth will open with a parable.
Our God once fed with manna and with birds,
And from a rock brought streams for Israel.
Yet more they sinned, provoking the Most High,
Forgetting cloud and fire in the wild.
They turned their hearts from God, failed to draw nigh,
Neglecting to share truths with every child.
But mercy brought them to the Holy Land,
Yet like their fathers, they chose to rebel.
And God brought justice with His mighty hand,
Rejected Jacob, and, on swords, priests fell.
   But from the sheepfolds, God raised up a king.
   And of God's mercy, David came to sing.

79

O God, they have defiled Your holy temple,
And Your inheritance is occupied.
For when Jerusalem began to tremble,
The nations asked if You withdrew to hide.
How long will You be angry, Lord, how long?
And will Your jealousy e'er burn like fire?
Pour out Your wrath, and show that You are strong.
To those who know You not, direct Your ire.
O God of our salvation, give Your aid.
Deliver us—atone for all our sin.
And for Your name, come let Your love pervade
In prisoners left to die who're chained within.
   Award our neighbors sevenfold their shame.
   Your pasture's sheep forever praise Your name.

80

Restore us, God, and let Your face come shine.
Shepherd of Israel, give Your ear and hear.
Come save us, LORD of hosts, regard Your vine
You planted; come restore and draw us near.
You brought this vine from Egypt by Your hand.
You drove out nations, cleared the chosen ground.
Deep root, it took, and filled Your fertile land,
And shaded mighty cedars all around.
Look down, O God, Your vine is burned with fire.
It's been cut down—Your vineyard, LORD—Your plant.
And by Your countenance, they will expire
Who praise You not, but come to You with cant.
  Restore us, LORD of hosts, for we are Thine.
  Come save us, God of hosts, let Your face shine.

81

Our strength is God; to Him we sing aloud.
We raise a song then sound the tambourine.
We heard Your answer from the thundercloud;
Your rescue came in our distress and need.
"O hear, My people, I will testify,
If you, O Israel, hearken unto Me;
I brought you out of Egypt, come comply
And take no other god, for I am He.
But Israel did not listen to My voice;
My people would not offer Me their praise;
They turned away—rebellion was their choice;
I gave them to their stubborn-hearted ways."
   O listen to our God; walk with our LORD
   That His rich blessings come—that they're outpoured.

82

Within the congregation of the mighty,
God stands before the gods to set things right.
"How long will you continue the unsightly
And rule in favor of this endless blight?
Defend the fatherless; uphold the poor;
Do justice to the destitute in need.
And rescue all the weak, for I implore
You free them from the wicked hand—take heed."
They know not and refuse to understand.
They walk in darkness; shaken is the earth.
"I said that you are gods, so take a stand
As sons of the Most High—that is your worth."
    Arise and judge the earth, O God, arise.
    Inherit all the nations and their skies.

83

Keep not Your silence, God, hold not Your peace—
And be not still. Your enemies, O God,
Have made an uproar; come and make them cease.
They raise their heads in hatred to maraud.
For they have taken crafty counsel on
Your people—schemed against Your treasured ones.
They plot to wipe them out; their plans are drawn.
Then Israel will have perished—and its sons.
O God, make them as chaff before the wind,
As fire burns the forest, as the flame
Sets fire to the mountains; they have sinned,
So let them be ashamed and seek Your name.
   That men may know that You are God alone.
   That Yahweh is Your name upon Your throne.

84

How lovely is Your dwelling place, O LORD,
And for Your glorious courts I long and yearn.
My heart and flesh will sing in one accord;
O living God, my joyful song discern.
For even humble sparrows find a home;
And for herself, a swallow to a nest,
Where she will place her young from gloam to gloam
Near altars, Thine, where mercy is expressed.
For better is one day, God, in Your courts
Than suffering a thousand days elsewhere.
Our God, a sun, a shield, who e'er supports,
Withholding no good thing from those who care.
  O LORD of hosts, Your face we long to see
  For bless'ed is the one who trusts in Thee.

85

O Lord, You showed Your favor to Your land,
Restored to Jacob his prosperity.
You took away their guilt and helped them stand;
Their sin You covered—each iniquity.
And You, O Lord, withdrew from them Your fury;
You turned from Your hot anger and Your wrath.
Restore us, God, come take away our worry.
Revive us, Lord, and place us on Your path.
O let me hear what God the Lord will speak.
Unto His saints, His people, He speaks peace.
But let them not be foolish; they are weak.
For those who fear Him, glory will not cease.
   Out of the ground springs up His faithfulness,
   And from the sky rains down His righteousness.

86

Incline Your ear, O LORD, and answer me
For I am poor and live in grievous need.
Preserve my life, be gracious, hear my plea.
You are my God I trust; I will concede.
And unto me be merciful, O Lord.
All day I call to You; come grant me joy.
For You, O Lord, are good and are adored,
Forgiving all who call without a ploy.
Teach me Your way, and help me walk in truth.
Unite my heart to fear Your holy name.
For I will praise Your name in heart and sooth.
Your steadfast love is great and brings You fame.
  For You are slow to anger, steadfast be.
  Give strength unto Your servant; comfort me.

87

A city stands upon the holy mount,
A city founded by our God of love,
Who, in His word, was clear in His account—
His love for Zion and its gates thereof.
For glorious things are spoken there, O God,
The city You created by Your hand.
You mentioned those who know You; You they laud,
The ones You know by name, born in Your land.
Though when the LORD shall count to list each person,
And as He makes His record, He will write:
"This one was born there," Zion calls him her son,
Who loves You, God, and shines Your loving light.
    The singers and the dancers likewise say,
      "Yea, all my springs are in Thee," on this day.

88

O LORD of my salvation, I have cried
All day and night before You; bend Your ear.
Come hear my prayer, allow me to confide
And spread my hands to You; O God, draw near.
My soul is full of troubles, and my life
Draws nigh unto the grave—so dark, so cold.
I have no strength; my heart is full of strife;
Unto the pit I come, distress untold.
O God, will You do wonders for the dead?
And will the dead arise to praise Your name?
And from the darkness, in this seat of dread,
Will righteousness prevail? Come take my shame.
  My morning prayers to You, O God, shall rise.
  Cast not my soul away to my demise.

89

A vision was once spoken to the loyal,
A warrior was given help from God,
And chosen from the people came a royal;
His name is David—shepherd, staff, and rod.
Anointed with My oil is My servant,
Established with My hand, and with My arm.
I've strengthened him, his faith is ever fervent,
His enemies shall not rise up to harm.
My firstborn shall be higher than all kings.
My steadfast love will keep him ever strong.
My covenant will stand, endures all things.
His offspring ever on the throne belong.
   Rebellion will be punished with the rod.
   My lovingkindness constant; I am God.

BOOK
FOUR

90

Before You made the mountains, earth, and world,
You've been our dwelling place; You've been our light.
Returned to dust is man, Your children hurled.
A thousand years to You is but a night.
Our secret sins are cast before You, Lord,
And all our days will pass under Your wrath.
Brief lives of toil and trouble are abhorred.
We fear Your anger, strayed we from Your path.
O teach us, Lord, to number all our days
That wisdom might take root within our hearts.
Return, O Lord, empathic are Your ways.
How long until Your loving mercy starts?
   Upon us shine Your beauty and Your favor,
   Establishing our works that shall not waver.

91

For he who dwells within the secret place
Of the Most High will evermore abide
Under the shadow of Almighty's grace,
Declaring faithful love to all beside.
And with His feathers He will cover thee;
Under His wings you will forever trust.
His truth will be your shield, and you will see
His angels will come keep you; He is just.
The terror of the night you will not fear,
Nor dread the arrow that will fly by day.
The pestilence in darkness won't come near,
Nor will destruction ever come your way.
  For I will answer him who calls on Me.
  Alongside in your trouble, I will be.

92

For it is good to praise the LORD and sing
Our thankfulness unto Your name, Most High.
Declare Your love at dawn, while worshipping;
Exalt You and Your faithfulness at night.
For You make me rejoice, e'en shout for joy
When I look on the great works of Your hands.
Magnificent and given to enjoy,
Your thoughts, profound—such beauty on Your lands.
The righteous thrive and grow much like Your trees
That flourish in the good house of the LORD.
They bear good fruit for ages in Thy breeze;
Their healthiness, by grace, is their reward.
  He is my Rock; the LORD our God is just.
  With no unrighteousness, in Him we trust.

93

The Lord reigns; He is robed in majesty
And clothed in strength and girded with His belt.
The world established in totality
Will not be moved; before Him are we knelt.
Your throne, O Lord, of old, establish'ed;
You are from everlasting, Holy God.
Your world You have created looks ahead
For in Your strength Your reign shall reach abroad.
The floods have lifted up, O Lord, they come
With lifted voices; we can hear them roar.
But mightier than thunder or the drum
Of waters is the power of the Lord.
   Your testimonies sure, and holiness
   Befits Your house; You dwell in righteousness.

94

O LORD, the God of vengeance, shine Your way;
Lift up thyself, O Judge o'er all the earth.
Repay the proud what they deserve this day
According to Your righteousness and worth.
O God, how long will wicked men exult?
And boast of wickedness in arrogance?
They break Your souls, Your legacy insult.
Withdrawn are they from Your inheritance.
They slay the widow and the foreigner;
The fatherless are murdered by their hand.
They say God cannot see; their sins recur;
The LORD will wipe them out and off the land.
 The LORD remains my stronghold and my rock.
 His comfort fills my heart; in it I walk.

95

O come and let us sing unto the LORD,
And let us make a joyful noise unto
The Rock of our salvation in accord.
Come in His presence, giving thanks anew.
Our LORD, above all gods, is God our King,
And in His hand He holds the depths of earth.
The heights of mountains, birthed from His wellspring,
The sea and land He formed; His voice gave birth.
O come and let us worship and submit
And kneel before our Maker; He is God.
The people of His pasture, though unfit,
Are sheep of holy hands of whom we laud.
  O harden not your heart to His still voice.
  Unlike at Meribah, turn and rejoice.

96

O sing unto the LORD; a new song sing.
O people of the earth sing unto Him.
And bless His name; He is our mighty King.
Declare salvation daily with a hymn.
His glory we declare among the heathen.
His works of wonder, share with everyone.
The LORD is great and praised in every season,
And feared above all gods the godly shun.
Ascribe to God, O families of the people,
Ascribe to God His glory and His strength.
Give glory to His name that lacks an equal.
Into His courts bring offerings at length.
  Let earth and sea exult, and all within.
  He comes to judge the earth and all therein.

97

The LORD reigns, so let all the earth rejoice!
Be glad, all coastlands, He reigns in the cloud,
Surrounded by thick darkness as His voice
Proclaims His righteousness while we are bowed.
For justice and uprightness are His throne;
And fire goes before Him, burns His foes.
His lightning shall illume; the earth is shown
And trembles in dismay when in the throes.
Yet light dawns for the righteous, for the saints,
And gladness for the upright, gentle heart.
Rejoice all in the LORD; remove constraints
And lift His name for He is set apart.
  For You, O LORD, are Most High o'er the earth,
  Above all gods, exalted, full of mirth.

98

O come and sing a new song to the LORD.
Great wonders He has done with His right hand.
Deliverance has come; His love outpoured,
His righteousness revealed upon the land.
Salvation is now known; His voice has called,
Along with steadfast love to Israel.
His faithfulness is shown; we stand enthralled.
His love displayed, affection filial.
O let the mighty sea resound and roar,
And all that fills it sing to holy God.
The mountains praise the King; from shore to shore
The rivers clap their hands, to Him applaud.
   The LORD shall come to judge the earth right soon
   With equity, come sing a joyful tune.

99

The LORD is great in Zion; He is seated
So high above the people who are lowly,
Above the cherubim and clouds, retreated.
An awe-inspiring name for He is holy.
The Mighty King loves justice; He is fair
And righteous on His throne, approach we slowly.
And at His footstool bow and offer prayer.
Exalt the LORD our God for He is holy.
They called upon His name, the priests of old,
For Moses, Aaron, Samuel trusted wholly.
And through a cloud He spoke of love untold.
Come worship at His mountain; He is holy.
  Their wrongdoings avenged, but e'er forgiven.
  He is a holy God, yet grace was given.

100

Come make a joyful noise unto the LORD!
And serve the LORD with gladness, all ye lands!
And in His presence sing in one accord.
Come praise Him as we lift up holy hands.
Acknowledge that the LORD is God above
For He has made us; praise Him—we are His.
We are His people formed by gracious love,
The sheep of His great pasture—beauteous.
And with thanksgiving, enter holy gates.
When in His courts give praise unto our King.
Give thanks to Him; a peaceful rest awaits.
We bless His name, unto our God we sing.
   The LORD is good; His mercy will ensure
   The truth of God forever will endure.

101

Of steadfast love and justice I will sing;
With music hear me lift my heart to Thee.
And of a blameless way I'm pondering.
O when will You, O LORD, come unto me?
And with integrity of heart I live
Within my house, for I will learn to walk
Away from evil hearts and will not give
Attention to what's vile or evil talk.
The faithful and the blameless I will favor
That they may dwell with me upon the land.
But those who work deceit, from virtue waver,
Are cut off and cast out by my command.
  For wicked hearts shall ever be abhorred
  And banished from the city of the LORD.

102

O LORD, my prayer, my cry, let come to Thee.
Hide not Your face from me this troubled day.
Incline Your ear to me, and You will see
Your answer's needed, LORD, do not delay.
I'm like a lonely sparrow on the roof.
I lie awake. My foes deride my name.
My days are like a shadow; Your reproof
Has thrown me down upon my face in shame.
O take me not away; this is my prayer
For I am in the midst of all my life.
Regard my destitution—be aware;
My days, God, do not shorten in my strife.
  You are the same; Your years shall have no end.
  To You, Your servants' children will ascend.

103

I bless the LORD; I bless His holy name.
And all that is within me, bless the LORD.
I bless the LORD, exalt and give acclaim.
And O my soul, I bless His name, adored.
As far as heavens rise above the earth,
All those who fear will see His love expressed.
All sins are cast away in our rebirth
As far as what is east spans from the west.
The everlasting mercy from His throne
Extends to all ye men who come with fear.
His righteousness to generations known,
Who keep His covenant, commandments near.
    Let all He has created praise the LORD,
    With angels of great strength, with hearts outpoured.

104

I bless You, LORD, You're clothed in majesty
And splendor; You alone can wear the light.
O LORD my God, I lift my soul to Thee.
You make the skies Your home and bring the night.
To mark the seasons, You have set the moon,
The sun aware which time at dusk to set.
You make the darkness night, when beasts commune.
The sun arises, lions cease their threat.
O may the glory of the LORD endure,
And may the LORD rejoice in all His deeds.
He, with a glance, can shake the verdant moor;
The mountains smoke when God's right hand proceeds.
   O let my meditation please the LORD.
   Let sinners and the wicked be no more.

105

He is the LORD, our God, who e'er recalls
His covenant with Abraham once given.
His oath freed prophets from their chains and walls.
To Israel, Canaan granted, clans were driven.
A famine He pronounced upon the land,
And Joseph sent, and sold, to be a slave,
A testing, laid with iron by His hand,
Release'ed by a king, his house to save.
His chosen servant Moses, sent to Ham
With Aaron, signs and wonders to be shown.
Ten plagues unleashed by God, the great I AM.
Provision made by bread of heaven, sown.

  He brought His people out with joy and song.
  His promise kept, we praise His name daylong.

106

Remember me, LORD, when You show Your favor;
And Your salvation—pray it visit me.
That I may see Your good that shall not waver,
For Your inheritance I long to see.
Our fathers, though delivered by Your hand,
Forgot Your works; Your counsel was not sought.
E'en though You turned the sea into dry land,
Your works of lovingkindness they forgot.
Yet Moses stood before You in the breach
To turn Your wrath away from foolish souls;
Still for an image of an ox they reached
And traded glory for their dying tolls.
  Though many times delivered, still within
  Their careless hearts they turned from You to sin.

BOOK
FIVE

107

Give thanks unto the LORD for He is good.
Recall those who once wandered in their thirst.
While ravenous for food, frail spirits stood
And cried to Him; He rescued the accursed.
And call to mind when others sat in gloom,
Imprisoned they, in chains, who had rebelled,
Who cried unto the LORD amidst their doom,
He saved them from distresses, darkness quelled.
Afflicted fools in their transgressions sighed
When they drew near unto the gates of death.
They cried unto the LORD, and He drew nigh
To send a word to heal them with His breath.
   E'en those who suffered tempests out at sea,
    When they cried out, He saved them lovingly.

108

O God, my heart is fixed, and I will sing;
Awake, O harp and lyre, to rouse the dawn.
I give You thanks with all that is my being;
I will rejoice for unto You I'm drawn.
Among the people, I will thank Your name.
Among the nations, I give praise to Thee.
Above the heavens rises Your great fame;
Your faithfulness will reach the clouds o'er me.
With Your right hand I pray You'll come give aid.
Deliver Your beloved—answer me.
And in His holiness, a promise made;
"These lands are Mine," He shouts triumphantly.
  Help us from trouble; aid from men is vain.
  With God we shall do valiantly and reign.

109

Hold not Your peace, O God, whom I revere,
Deceitful mouths are open unto me.
Their lying tongues encircle me to jeer
With words of hatred; prithee, hear my plea.
My love's returned with animus and spite,
Yet I will give myself unto my prayer.
For they rewarded me with harm outright,
Though from my heart and hand came love and care.
O help me, LORD my God, and liberate
According to Your mercy; move Your hand.
Although they curse, You bless, for You are great.
My adversaries, clothe with shame, disband.
   For with my mouth the LORD I greatly praise.
   He stands next to the poor, his soul to raise.

110

The LORD says to My Lord, come now and sit
At My right hand; be seated near, abreast,
Until I make Your enemies submit
To be Your footstool at Your LORD's behest.
Your mighty scepter Yahweh sends from Zion;
Go rule Your enemies who're in Your midst.
Your people will be willing, each Your scion,
In holy garments for Your day t'enlist.
The LORD has sworn an oath He won't revoke,
In order of Melchizedek the priest.
For on the day of wrath He will invoke
His judgment of the greatest to the least.
  For of the brook He will drink in the way,
  And lift His head to rise above the fray.

III

O I will praise the LORD with my whole heart.
I praise the LORD in upright company.
Majestic are His works, and set apart;
His righteousness endures eternally.
Remembered are the wonders He has made;
Compassionate and gracious is our LORD.
For those who fear, His sustenance will aid.
His covenant will never be ignored.
The LORD has shown the power of His deeds;
Inheritance of th'nations He bequeathed.
And each commandment from His throne proceeds
With verity and justice; they're enwreathed.
   The dawn of wisdom is the fear of God.
   Insight attends all those who kneel and nod.

112

O bless'ed is the man who fears the LORD;
In His commandments he will find delight.
His offspring in the land see grace outpoured—
Their generation mighty and upright.
For wealth and riches will be in his home.
His righteousness shall persevere fore'er.
For light dawns in the darkness and the gloam
For upright souls; His mercy meets them there.
The one who lends, whose exploits are but just—
Who gives unto the poor who are in need—
Will not be shaken; in Him is his trust,
His heart established, fear will not succeed.
   The wicked man will see the righteous rise,
    While his desires fall in his demise.

113

O servants of the LORD, we praise His name,
And bless'ed be His name forevermore.
From this time forth, we shall with praise proclaim
The name of Yahweh—ever to adore.
And from the rising of the sun at dawn
Until its setting at the close of day,
His name be lifted up; we call upon
The matchless name of God, who we obey.
For who is like the LORD, our God on high,
Who looks far down on th'heavens and on earth?
For from the dust He raises those who cry,
Lifts from the dunghill nobles in His worth.
   The barren, when she calls upon His name,
    Will have her own to love, a home to claim.

114

When Israel went out from captivity,
The house of Jacob left Egyptian land.
And into Judah refuge was to be.
For Israel, His dominion was at hand.
The sea looked on and fled; the Jordan turned,
The mountains skipped like rams, the hills like lambs.
Why did you flee, O sea, why so concerned?
And mountains, hills, why skip like lambs and rams?
O tremble at the presence of the Lord;
The God of Jacob shakes the earth and all.
He turned the flint into a spring that poured,
A rock into a flowing waterfall.
  For God delivered Israel with His hand—
  Came through the desert to the Promised Land.

115

Not unto us, O Lord, not unto us,
But to Your name give glory, God above.
And for Your steadfast love and faithfulness,
For Your truth's sake we trust You and Your love.
Why should the nations say, "Where is their God?"
Our God is in the heavens, e'er will be.
He does all that He pleases, no facade,
While nations forge their idols ignorantly.
But Israel, may you be forever blessed
By God, who made the heavens and the earth.
The dead do not give praise; nor will they rest
As they descend to silent death and dearth.
   But we will bless the Lord forevermore.
   He is our help and shield, now as before.

116

I love the LORD for He has heard my call
And has inclined His ear unto my voice.
His mercy, my appeal; He is my all;
As long as I have breath, I will rejoice.
The snares of death and gloom encompassed me.
The pangs of Sheol overwhelmed my soul.
I called upon His name; He heard my plea.
"LORD, save me," was my cry, "come make me whole."
From death You have delivered me, O LORD,
My eyes from tears, my feet from stumbling.
And in the land of th'living, Thy reward:
Before Thee I will walk in thanksgiving.
  Salvation's cup will I lift up to Thee;
  Receive my vows for all the world to see.

117

O praise the LORD, all nations; give Him praise!
Extol Him all ye people. Hallelu!
His steadfast love is great for us all days.
Endures forever, faithful love so true.
  O praise the LORD, all nations; praise His name!
  Come praise the LORD, and give our LORD acclaim!

118

Give thanks unto the LORD, for He is good;
The faithful love of God endures forever.
Let Israel, Aaron, all who fear, and should,
Choose speaking of His love as their endeavor.
I called unto the LORD while in distress,
And in a spacious place He set me free.
I will not fear, for He draws near to bless;
His help will make the wicked turn and flee.
Far better to take refuge in the LORD
Than trust in man or nobles who are weak.
His right hand raised, His discipline outpoured.
He is my strength and song—the One I seek.
   Rejected stone, our cornerstone, was laid.
   Rejoice, this is the day the LORD has made.

119

The law of Yahweh charts a blameless walk;
Obey His just decrees, and life is blessed.
His precepts seek with all your heart, and talk
With lips that put forth praise; of Him attest.
Your word is treasured deep within my heart
That I might turn from sin; Your judgments teach
To keep a young man pure, statutes impart
The way revealed, commands I should not breach.
Your precepts let me walk at liberty;
Your testimonies I will share with kings;
Your law, at night, keeps me from misery,
And of Your promises my tongue e'er sings.
  The revelation of Your words gives light,
  For Your instruction is my heart's delight.

120

Unto the LORD I cried in my distress.
He heard and answered my song of degrees.
Deliver me, O LORD, for they oppress,
Their lips and tongues that lie and cheat with ease.
For what else shall be given unto thee?
And what else, may I question, shall be done?
A warrior's sharp arrows shall it be?
Or coals of juniper, deceitful tongue?
What misery, I sojourn in Meshech,
And in the tents of Kedar I so dwell,
For I have lived too long as but a fleck
With those who hate His peace; I hear the knell.
  I am for peace, and turmoil I deplore,
  But when I speak, those near declare for war.

121

I lift my eyes unto the mountainside.
Where will I look for help while in my dearth?
My help is from the LORD, who comes beside;
The Maker of the heavens and the earth.
For He will not allow your foot to slip
And will not slumber, He who will protect.
The LORD, your keeper, will not lose His grip;
Providing shelter, He will not neglect.
The sun will never strike you in the day,
Nor will the moon bring torment in the night.
The evil in the earth begets dismay,
Yet He will keep you from its harm and blight.
  The LORD will keep your going out and in
    From this time forth; He'll shelter you from sin.

122

When they said unto me all that awaits
Within the house of God, how glad my heart.
Our feet are standing in its city gates—
Jerusalem, a city set apart.
The tribes of Israel thank His holy name
As they go up to follow His decree.
The thrones of judgment set for His acclaim,
The house of David reigns eternally.
Pray for the peace of dear Jerusalem.
May there be peace within your city walls.
Prosperity within—none to condemn
Within your palaces and in your halls.
   "Within thee, come thee peace," I will now say.
   Because of His good house, let good give way.

123

For unto You, O LORD, I lift my eyes—
The One enthroned in heaven, LORD our God.
Just as a watchful servant who is wise,
I look to see the LORD of whom I'm awed.
Alerted eyes take heed of You, O LORD,
Until Your mercy comes upon our lives.
Show us Your favor; all will be restored;
We watch until Your charity arrives.
Enough contempt, O LORD, we wait for Thee.
Deliver us from scorn, from those at ease.
The proud show disregard exceedingly;
Our song, a song of mercy and degrees.
  Our eyes are ever watchful for Your hand;
  Show us Your favor, LORD, at Your command.

124

For had the LORD not been upon our side,
May Israel say, if Yahweh was not near
When people rose against us like a tide
In burning anger, we would not be here.
The waters would have swept us all away;
The torrent would have come to drown our souls;
The deluge would have ended us that day
If absent was the One Israel extols.
O bless'ed be the LORD who set us free,
Who gave us not as prey into their teeth.
For as a bird we have escaped to be
Free from the fowler's snare set from beneath.
  Our help is in the good name of the LORD,
  Creator of the earth and skies that soar.

125

For those who trust in God are like Mount Zion,
Which cannot be removed, for'er abides.
And like Jerusalem, beneath Orion,
His people He surrounds, like its hillsides.
The scepter of the wicked shall not rest
Upon the land allotted to the righteous,
Lest they put forth their hands like the oppressed
And turn unto themselves as do the lightless.
Do what is good, O Lord, unto the good—
To those with upright hearts who turn to Thee.
But those whose ways are crooked never should
Believe the Lord will ever set them free.
   Upon fair Israel peace shall come for aye
   As all who trust in Yahweh can rely.

126

We were like those who dream when God restored
We captive ones of Zion to our home.
Our mouths were filled with laughter when our Lord
Received our shouts of joy and songs: Shalom!
"The Lord has done great things for them," they said
Among the nations who beheld our plight.
The Lord has done great things for us who fled
From life, as the displaced, exiled outright.
Restore our fortunes, Lord, like southern streams.
For they shall reap with joy what's sown in tears.
And he who goes out weeping as beseems
A contrite heart returns without his fears.
   When going forth with weeping precious seeds,
   He shall rejoice when bringing in the sheaves.

127

Unless the LORD is counted as the builder,
Then they who build the house labor in vain.
And any effort will at length bewilder
Unless the LORD will go before their gain.
It is in vain for you to rise up early,
Or sit up late, or watch the city gates,
Or eat the bread prepared in hurly-burly;
For to the ones He loves, good sleep awaits.
Behold, our children, our inheritance
From Yahweh—sons are but a sweet reward.
Like arrows to great warriors, advance
These gifts to mankind given by our LORD.
  How blessed is he whose quiver doth elate
  The man with adversaries at his gate.

128

For everyone is blessed who fears the LORD;
According to His ways, the happy walk.
By labor of his hands he can afford
To feast on what is good and on good stock.
Your wife shall be just like a fruitful vine;
Your children like fine youthful olive trees.
Behold, thus shall it be when the divine
Extends His blessings to those on their knees.
For out of Zion comes His goodness, rife
With blessings for all who will walk with Him.
For you will see the good come in this life—
Unto His land, unto Jerusalem.
   Your children's children shall be your increase,
   And unto Israel, let there come His peace.

129

"How often, since my youth, affliction came,"
Let Israel say, "They have yet to prevail;
How often, since my youth, came they to maim."
Let Israel say, "Our God has made them fail.
Upon my back the plowers plowed to hurt,
Their furrows long, yet by His grace I stand."
The LORD is righteous, able to subvert
And cut the wicked's ropes they have at hand.
Let those who hate fair Zion be turned back
And be confounded, shamed in their disgrace.
As grass upon the housetops in their lack,
With roots that wither, sheaves one can't embrace.
  For never shall their passersby declare,
  "We bless you in His name; this is our prayer."

130

Out of the depths have I cried unto Thee;
Please hear my voice, O Lord, ere I lose heart.
And let Your ears be heedful to my plea;
Without Your mercy, hope will soon depart.
If You considered all iniquities,
Then who could stand before one so revered?
But with You is forgiveness to appease
Our sinfulness that You, Lord, might be feared.
And for the Lord I wait, my soul will wait;
I place all of my hope upon His word.
More than the morning's watchmen at the gate,
More than the watchmen, I wait to be heard.
   Let Israel seek redemption from the Lord,
   His faithful love abundantly outpoured.

131

O Lord, within my heart find not vain pride,
Nor haughtiness when You look in my eyes.
For if I lift my heart or turn aside,
My countenance speaks lofty compromise.
But I have calmed and quieted my soul,
And cast aside vainglorious pursuits.
By faith I yield my heart and eyes, make whole
The rest of me—more like Your attributes.
Much like a mother's child, so am I.
Much like a mother's child who's been weaned,
By faith I turn; on You I shall rely
While trading vanity for the serene.
    O Israel, place your hope upon the Lord—
    From this time forth until forevermore.

132

O LORD, remember David and recall
The oath unto the Mighty One he vowed,
And all of his afflictions while in thrall
To enemies; e'en sleep he disallowed.
"For I shall not step foot in my abode,
Or go into my bed until I see
A dwelling place for God to be bestowed
Unto the Mighty One of Jacob's glee."
The LORD swore unto David a sure oath
From which He shall not turn—His good command:
"For if this covenant in solemn troth
Is followed by your sons, your throne will stand."
  The LORD chose Zion as His resting place,
  And David's crown will ever shine of grace.

133

Behold, all souls, how good and pleasant is
Dear life when brothers dwell in unity!
Why anguish, you, in strife? Consider His
Commanded blessings for eternity.
For harmony is like an oil that's fine,
An ointment used upon thy head, thy crown.
And running down the beard it flows like wine,
Like Aaron's beard, onto his robes—streams down.
For unity is like the dew of Hermon
That falls upon the mountainsides of Zion.
For unity and peace—hear this, my sermon—
For brotherhood and for your loving scion.
    For in fair Zion He commands this blessing.
    For life forevermore, peace He's expressing.

134

Behold, bless ye the LORD; come give Him praise,
All servants of the LORD who stand by night!
Within His sanctuary, stand agaze,
And lift up holy hands with hearts contrite!
  O may the LORD, from Zion, bless your soul,
   Who made the earth and made the heavens whole.

135

O praise the LORD, all servants, praise His name!
And all who stand within His house give praise!
All in the courts of God, give Him acclaim.
To praise His name is pleasant; praise His ways!
For I know that the LORD our God is great;
Above all other gods, how great is He.
In heaven and on earth, what doth elate
Our LORD, He does—as well in sky and sea.
He lifts the clouds and fires bolts in rain,
And sends the mighty wind across the sky.
Delivered Israel from Egyptian pain,
Struck down the mighty kings who dared defy.
   Vain idols made of silver and of gold
    Shall never stand with Zion's King of old.

136

Give thanks unto the Lord for He is good,
His mercy and His love endure forever.
Give thanks unto the God of gods—all should,
His mercy and His love endure forever.
Give thanks unto the Lord of lords with mirth,
His mercy and His love endure forever.
To Him who made the heavens and the earth,
His mercy and His love endure forever.
To Him who made the sun to give us light,
His mercy and His love endure forever.
To Him who made the moon and stars for night,
His mercy and His love endure forever.
  Give thanks unto the Lord, for now and ever.
  His mercy and His love endure forever.

137

In exile we sat by their rivers cold,
And in remembrance, wept of our fair home.
We hung our lyres on their willows old,
Without a song to sing when forced to roam.
For there our captors voiced a cruel demand
To sing our songs of Zion while confined:
"Rejoice and lift your praises of your land!"
How can we sing His song when so maligned?
Jerusalem, if I fail to recall
My love for you, then let my right hand fail,
And render my tongue useless, stuck withal.
If not my joy, then judge me on thy scale.
   Remember Babylon, O Lord, be just.
   Advance Your retribution—we will trust.

138

I give You thanks, O LORD, with my whole heart.
Before the gods will I sing praise to Thee.
I'll give thanks to Your name that's set apart,
And toward Your holy temple bend my knee.
Your steadfast love, Your faithfulness, and truth
Be praised; Your name and word exalted high.
And when I cried You answered me in sooth,
My strength of soul increased—I testify.
And all the kings of earth shall praise You, LORD,
When they hear of Your promises and words.
For they shall sing of You with hearts outpoured.
Of Your great glory, they shall sing like birds.
  You will preserve me and extend Your hand.
  You will fulfill my purpose as You've planned.

139

For You, O LORD, have searched me, and You know
When I sit down and when I rise again.
From far away You know my thoughts although
The sum of Yours I cannot comprehend.
And You observe my travels and my rest;
You are acquainted with all of my ways.
Before a word is on my tongue, attest,
You know it altogether—every phrase.
I cannot flee Your presence; You are there
In Sheol and in heaven's colonnade.
Your hand will lead and hold me; I'm aware
How fearfully and wonderfully I'm made.
  O search me, God, and know my heart, I pray
  You'll lead me in the everlasting way.

140

Deliver me, O LORD, from evil men
With violent hearts conspiring out of spite.
They gather, stir up wars time and again,
With sharp tongues and with venom in their bite.
Protect me, LORD, from violent, wicked hands—
The prideful who spread nets along the path.
They set their snares to trap me in their plans.
You are my God; come take them in Your wrath.
I call for help; attend unto my cry.
O LORD, You are my Savior and my strength.
Grant not their vile desires, LORD, deny
Malicious schemes the wicked plot at length.
  The LORD upholds the just cause of the poor.
  With praise we shall dwell with You evermore.

141

I call upon You, LORD, hasten to me.
Give ear unto my voice, I call to You.
Come count my prayer as incense, and to Thee
I lift my hands in sacrifice anew.
And set a guard over my mouth, O LORD.
Protect my heart from any evil thing.
For those with malice, sowing their discord,
I pray You stave them off, my God, my King.
But let the righteous strike me; it is kind,
As his rebuke is oil for my head.
And let me not refuse, but be aligned.
I pray against the evil, whom I dread.
   I look to You, yet those with hearts awry
    Will fall in their own nets while I pass by.

142

Unto the LORD I cry out with my voice;
I plead for mercy with my voice aloud
And pour out my complaint—my only choice—
Reveal my troubles to Him while I'm bowed.
LORD, when my spirit faints You know my way.
For on this path I walk they laid a snare.
Look to the right and see, to my dismay,
My refuge failed; no one for me is there.
Attend unto my cry for I am low.
Deliver me from persecutors for
They are too strong for me, of this I know.
Set free my soul—this prison I deplore.
   That I may give You thanks and praise Your name.
   The righteous will surround me in my shame.

143

LORD, hear my prayer; come listen to my plea.
Withhold Your rightful judgment; hear my plight.
And in Your righteousness come answer me,
For none alive are righteous in Your sight.
The enemy pursues me; I am weak.
For with dismay my heart is overcome,
Crushed to the ground, my circumstances bleak.
I dwell in darkness like the dead; I'm numb.
I trust in You; reveal which way to go.
I long for You; hide not Your face from me.
Come teach me; show Your will, and I will know
How I can walk on level ground with Thee.
　　Because of Your great name, LORD, let me live.
　　Deliver me in righteousness—forgive.

144

The LORD, my Rock, be praised; He is my shield.
He trains my hands for battle and for war.
He is my fortress; in Him I'm concealed.
He is my steadfast love forevermore.
Yet what is man, LORD, that You care for him?
The son of man that You will give him thought?
For man is like a breath, his end but grim,
Who passes like a shadow all for naught.
Come bow Your heavens, LORD, make Your way down,
And touch the mountains—they shall put forth smoke.
Send lightning, strew my enemies around,
And set me free—their falsehood come uncloak.
  LORD, bless our children, storehouses, and land.
  How blessed are all who turn to You to stand.

145

I will exalt You, God, my King forever—
Lift up Your name to praise You every day.
To give You honor is my one endeavor—
For You are great, and unto You I pray.
Your works are wonderful and glorious,
And I will speak of splendor that is Thine.
Your awe-inspiring works too numerous—
To list them all is futile; I resign.
The LORD helps all who fall—and the oppressed.
All eyes will turn to You to seek provision.
For all Your ways are gracious, I attest,
Your hand will open—blessings in due season.
  My mouth will speak the praises of the LORD.
  All bless His holy name in one accord.

146

Sing hallelujah! Praise the LORD, my soul!
Yes I will praise the LORD all of my days.
And while I have my being I'll extol
The LORD and sing His praises for always.
Trust not in nobles—man, who cannot save—
For when his breath departs, his plans will end.
But happy is the man whose heart he gave
Unto the LORD, on whom he can depend.
The LORD gives sight unto the blinded eyes,
And raises up all those who are oppressed.
The hungry fed; the low He will help rise;
The fatherless and widows will be blessed.
  Sing hallelujah! God, O Zion, reigns!
  All generations—He will break your chains.

147

Sing hallelujah! Sing unto our God!
For it is good to give our LORD our praise.
With thankful hearts and instruments applaud
Him who commands the sun to come ablaze.
The LORD rebuilds Jerusalem and heals
The brokenhearted, binding up their wounds.
He gathers outcasts, granting their appeals.
Afflicted hearts He helps; He is attuned.
Yet God is not impressed with man or horse;
Their pow'r and strength are weak when seen above.
The LORD is pleased with those who plot their course
By fearing Him, their hope is His great love.
   Sing hallelujah! Israel, you are blessed.
   His word, in love, to Jacob was professed.

148

Sing hallelujah! Give Yahweh all praise!
From soaring heavens and the highest heights,
His angels and His hosts, with eyes agaze,
Will praise His name and hold Him in their sights.
The sun, the moon, and all you shining stars,
By His command, created to endure;
And waters held in heaven's reservoirs
All praise Him and all held in His allure.
And from the earth, all monsters in the deep,
The lightning, hail, and snow and wind and cloud,
Creation, cattle, men and women, sheep—
Let them give praise to God and sing aloud!
  Sing hallelujah! Israel's God be praised!
  Our God, for thee, a horn His hand has raised.

149

Sing hallelujah! Sing a song that's new!
Praise Him in the assembly of the holy!
Let Israel celebrate its Maker, who
All Zion's children praise—King of the lowly!
Come give Him praise with music and with dancing;
Make melodies with tambourine and lyre.
Be joyful, saints, His glory is advancing,
And sing upon your beds with hearts afire.
Let praises of our God be in their throats
As two-edged swords find way into their hands.
The nations will be punished; He devotes
To bind their kings in chains—His justice stands.
  Sing hallelujah, all beneath the steeple.
  This is the honor for His godly people.

150

Sing hallelujah! Praise our Lord our God,
And in His sanctuary give God praise!
And in His mighty heavens, vast and broad,
We praise our holy God all of our days.
Come praise Him for His mighty acts and deeds.
According to His greatness, praise His name.
And with the trumpet sound His praise proceeds;
With harp and lyre we praise and give acclaim.
We praise Him with a tambourine and dance.
We praise Him with stringed instruments and flute.
We praise Him with loud cymbals that enhance
Our praise unto our God that's resolute.
  Sing hallelujah! Praise in one accord!
   Let everything that breathes come praise the Lord!

Printed in the United States
by Baker & Taylor Publisher Services